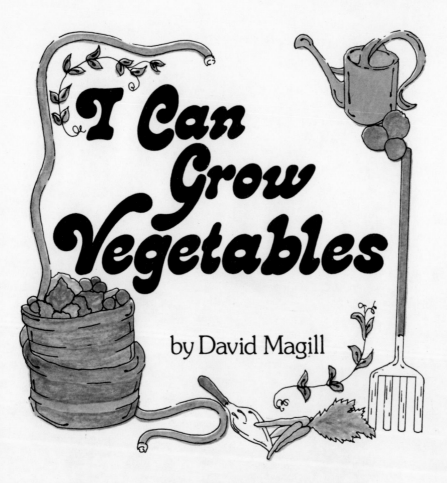

I Can Grow Vegetables

by David Magill

illustrated by Karen Sukoneck

DANDELION BOOKS
Published by Dandelion Press, Inc.

Wouldn't you like to be able to grow vegetables that you can eat? If you would, you can. If you haven't ever done it before, you may not know how easy it is, or how much fun. This book will tell you exactly what you must do to raise three kinds of vegetables—radishes, carrots, and string beans (snap beans). They're good choices for the first-time vegetable gardener because they are all simple to grow. But once you've raised a crop of these three, you'll be ready to go on to others: lettuce, peas, tomatoes, corn—almost anything that can grow in your part of the country.

Not only is it easy and fun to grow your own vegetables, but

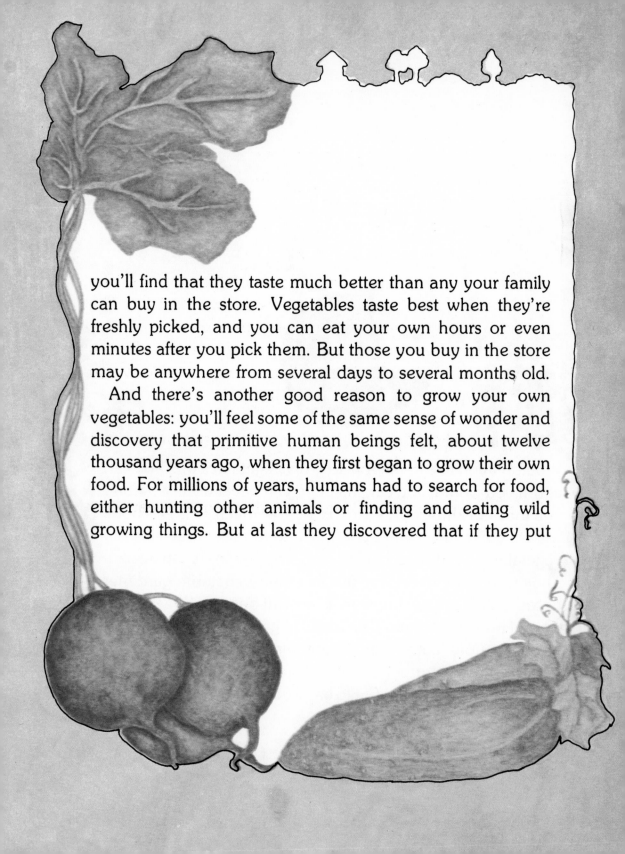

you'll find that they taste much better than any your family can buy in the store. Vegetables taste best when they're freshly picked, and you can eat your own hours or even minutes after you pick them. But those you buy in the store may be anywhere from several days to several months old.

And there's another good reason to grow your own vegetables: you'll feel some of the same sense of wonder and discovery that primitive human beings felt, about twelve thousand years ago, when they first began to grow their own food. For millions of years, humans had to search for food, either hunting other animals or finding and eating wild growing things. But at last they discovered that if they put

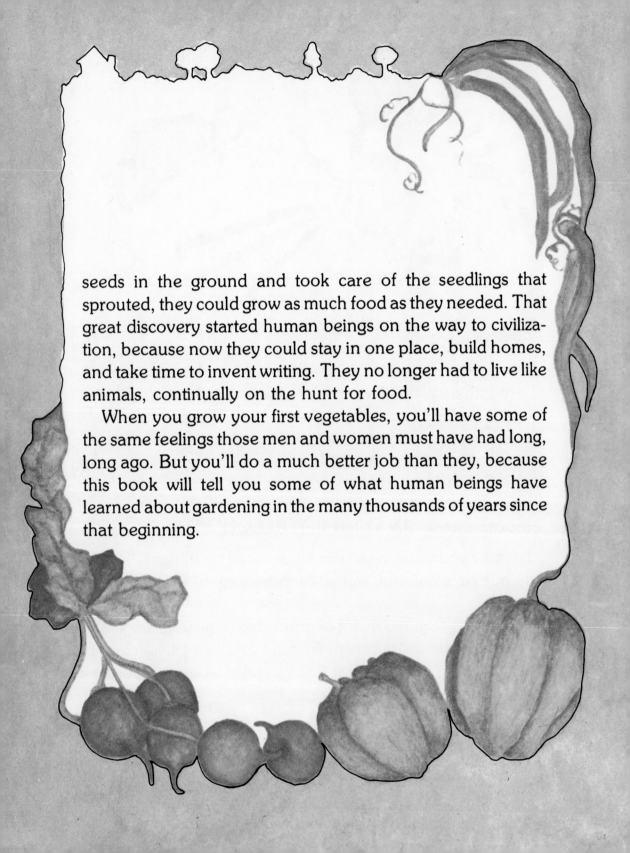

seeds in the ground and took care of the seedlings that sprouted, they could grow as much food as they needed. That great discovery started human beings on the way to civilization, because now they could stay in one place, build homes, and take time to invent writing. They no longer had to live like animals, continually on the hunt for food.

When you grow your first vegetables, you'll have some of the same feelings those men and women must have had long, long ago. But you'll do a much better job than they, because this book will tell you some of what human beings have learned about gardening in the many thousands of years since that beginning.

SIX THINGS YOU'LL NEED

To grow your own vegetables, you need six things—some of them free, some not, but all of them easy to find. Here they are:

1. *Soil*. You need a plot of ground to grow your vegetables in. It must be soil—not plain sand and not sticky clay, but brown earth, the kind that turns to mud when it is very wet.

Your first garden won't take up much room. A square piece of ground, 5 feet wide and 5 feet deep (from front to back), will be large enough. If your back yard or side yard doesn't have room for a plot of that size and shape, you can make your garden long and narrow: 12 feet long and 2 feet from front to back. Measure out the garden plot with a yardstick, tape measure, or even a ruler. Stick little wooden stakes or twigs into the ground at the corners, so you can see just where to dig and to plant.

2. *Sun*. You must pick a place that will get sunshine all day or at least most of the day. Without the energy of sunlight, the plants can't turn water and plant food into stalks, leaves, roots, and fruit.

3. *Seeds*. Any garden shop or variety store and many a hardware store has vegetable seeds for sale. They come in little envelopes, and are usually displayed in racks. Pick out one packet of radishes, one of carrots, and one of string beans (make sure they're "pole beans," not "bush beans"). If there is more than one variety of each in the rack, read the envelopes and pick the ones you like best. Some radishes, for instance, have a hot or spicy flavor, while others are mild. Most young people like the mild ones, while many adults

like the spicy ones. The best radishes for your garden are the small, round, red kind, not the big red ones or the long white ones.

4. *Fertilizer*. Most soils don't have enough plant food in them; it gets used up or washed out over the years. So you'll need to add fertilizer to the soil. There are many kinds. The best fertilizers, for many reasons, are natural or organic materials such as horse manure or cow manure. But since not many people live near a stable or dairy farm, the easiest thing to do is buy a 5-pound or 10-pound bag or box of fertilizer at a garden shop or hardware store. *Make sure it's for vegetable gardens, not for trees or evergreens*; it will say on the label what it is meant to be used on. You can also use "general purpose" plant food for your vegetable garden.

If you can, buy a plant food that's made of organic materials. It will say "organic" on the box or bag. If you can't find one that's organic, buy an inorganic plant food—but, again, make sure it's labeled either "for vegetables" or "general purpose."

5. *Water*. There must be a faucet near your garden plot, because you can't depend on rain. You will also need a fine-spray watering can or, even better, a hose.

6. *Tools*. For a small vegetable plot, only a few tools are necessary. You can borrow the first three, because you will use them only the first day or two. They're a pointed shovel, a spading fork, and a rake.

shovel

spading fork

rake

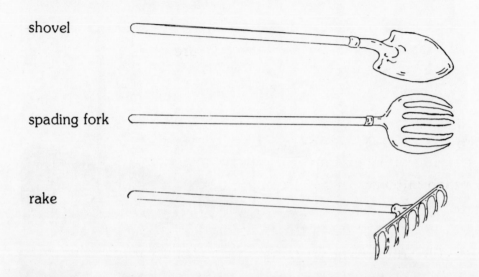

But all through the growing season you'll need two others, so you'd better get your own—a trowel and a cultivator.

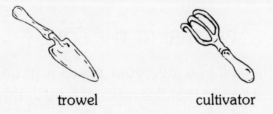

trowel   cultivator

Also, for your beans—which grow up poles—you will need 10 sticks or poles about as tall as a tall man. Any smooth, round poles will do—even saplings or dead branches that you find in nearby woods. If you can't find any, you can buy them at the same store that sells seeds.

PREPARING THE SOIL

Loosening the soil. To give your seeds a good home, you must loosen the soil so that the roots can push through it, and so that water and air can work their way down from the surface. But don't start until it's planting time in your part of the country. In the cooler northern half of the United States, that means mid-April for radishes and carrots, and early May for the beans. In warmer southern states, you can start a month or so earlier.

To loosen the soil, use the shovel or the spading fork, whichever works better in your soil. Shove it into the ground with your foot; then push the handle down so it turns up a big shovelful or forkful of soil. Turn it over and hit the soil a few times with the shovel or fork until all the lumps or clods are broken up. (If your garden plot has thick grass growing on it, you may need help from an adult to push the shovel down through the grass and then slice off the top, but once the grass is gone, you can manage the rest yourself.) Loosen the earth at least eight or nine inches down—about as deep as this book is long. It's hard work and takes time—but it's the biggest single job you have to do, and once it's done, the rest is easy.

Incidentally, when you turn over the soil, if you find that it's almost all sand, you'll have to buy one other thing—a small bag of *peat moss*, a dried, crumbly, papery stuff. Sand won't hold water or plant food, but peat moss will. Spread five or ten pounds of peat moss over your garden, and mix it into the soil. But if your soil is brown earth, and if it makes a good solid mud when you wet it, you don't need peat moss.

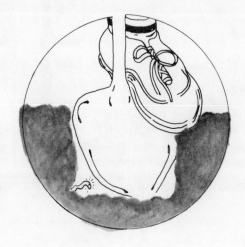

Clearing the ground. When you are turning the soil, you'll come across twigs, stones, roots, broken glass, and other things that don't belong in your garden. Pick them out, or rake them out, and throw them away.

Pulverizing and leveling the soil. Hold the rake with the handle straight up and down. Now bang down gently all over the garden plot. This will break up little clods and turn them into fine soil. Then turn the rake over so you can drag the back of it over the surface of the garden; that way, you can easily level out little hills and valleys until the garden is as flat as a tabletop.

Fertilizing. Now you are ready to fertilize your soil. As with any food, too little isn't good—and neither is too much. So measure it carefully. If you are using an organic plant food,

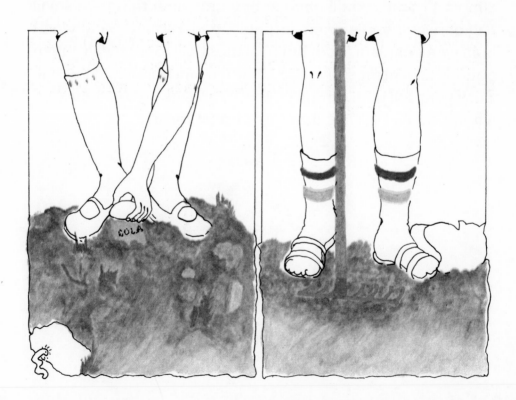

you will probably need about three cupfuls for the whole plot. If you are using an inorganic plant food, you may need only about a cupful. But to make sure, look on the package label for instructions, or ask an adult to look and to figure out for you how much to use.

A good way to spread the fertilizer is to measure out the right amount into a pail or coffee can, then scoop up a little at a time in your trowel and scatter it over the ground. After you have spread the fertilizer, rake gently back and forth to mix it into the top of the soil.

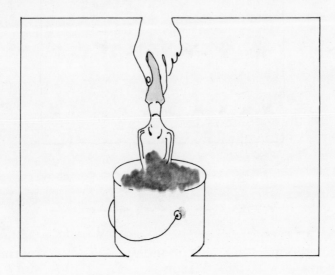

PLANTING

You're almost ready to plant your seeds.

Almost, because you haven't yet decided which seeds will go where. To decide that, you must see where the sun is in the sky most of the day. The beans will grow tall, and you don't want them to cut off the sunlight from the carrots or radishes. So the beans must be on the north side of the plot, and the lower-growing carrots and radishes on the south side, where they'll get the sun. Also, where you plant the seeds will depend on what shape your garden is—whether you have a 5-by-5 square or a 12-by-2 rectangle.

Here's your garden plan if you have a 5-by-5 plot (imagine you're looking down on the garden from upstairs).

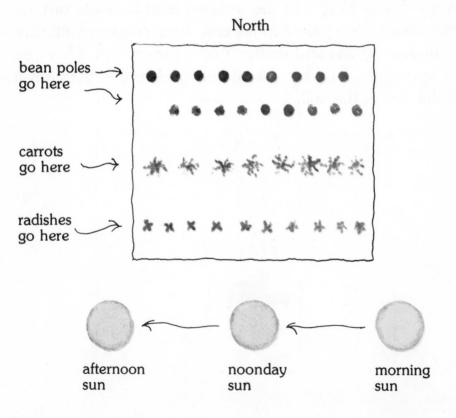

And here's your plan if your garden is 12-by-2:

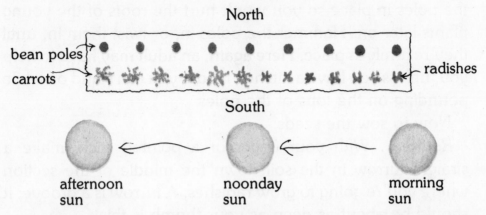

If you can't lay out your garden plot this way because it's long and narrow and has to run from north to south, then here is your plan:

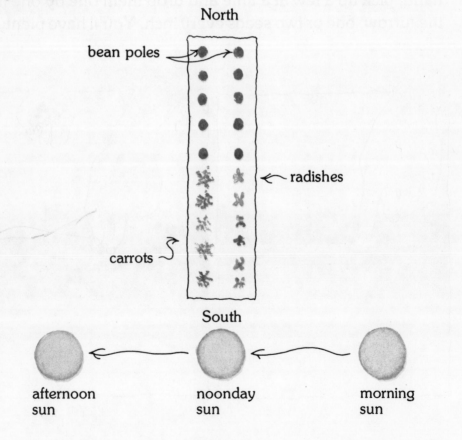

One more thing. Before planting the beans, it's best to put the poles in place so you won't hurt the roots of the young plants later on. Hammer the poles in, or twist them in, until they're firmly in place. Here again, an adult may have to help you, unless you have a kitchen ladder you can stand on while pounding on the tops of the poles.

Now to sow the seeds:

Radishes. With your finger or a pointed stick, make a straight furrow in the soil down the middle of the section where you're going to grow radishes. A furrow is a groove; it should be about as deep as your thumb is thick.

Now open the seed packet, and put some of the little round seeds in the palm of your hand. With the fingers of your other hand, pick up a few at a time and drop them one by one into the furrow, one or two seeds every inch. You'll have plenty of

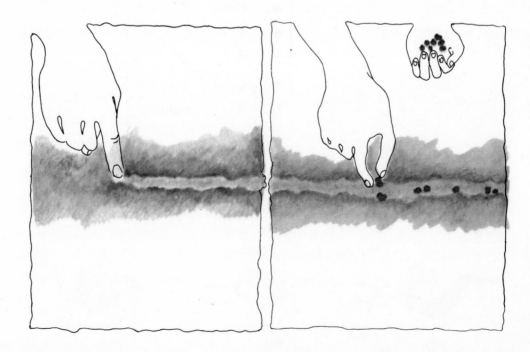

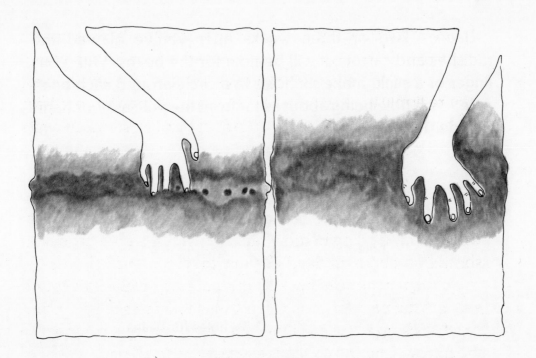

seeds left in the packet; that's fine, because radishes grow quickly and you'll plant them a second time in a few weeks, after you've eaten the first crop.

When you have sown seeds all along the furrow, push soil on top of the seeds, covering them about as deep as your thumb is thick. Press down gently with your palms all along the covered row, to make the soil somewhat firm where the seeds are.

That's it. You've planted your radishes!

Carrots. Make a furrow and sow the seeds just as you did the radishes. Carrot seeds are smaller and harder to handle, and you may have trouble dropping them in only one at a time. Don't worry about it. Later on, when too many come up, you'll pull out the extras; we call that "thinning" the seedlings.

Beans. Two or three weeks after you've planted the radishes and carrots, it will be time for the beans. With your finger or a stick, make six holes in a circle around each bean pole, each hole being about as far from the pole as your hand is wide. It will look like this:

pole

holes for beans

Each hole should be an inch or so deep. Drop one bean into each hole; make sure it goes down. Cover it with earth, and press the earth down.

WATERING AND WAITING

Every time you plant seeds, water them immediately. Use a fine spray, not a strong or heavy one, and not a solid stream; that would wash the seeds out.

How much water is enough? You want the soil to soak it up and to get wet down below, not just on the surface. When the top looks quite wet and little puddles begin to appear, stop watering; dig up one little spot where there are no seeds to see how the earth is underneath, an inch or two down. If it's dry, water some more, using a slow, fine spray. Once you get used to watering, you'll know how much is enough, just by the look of the surface.

So now your seeds are planted and the soil is wet. Next morning you rush out to see—and you see nothing! That afternoon, home from school, you rush out to see—and see nothing! And that's the way it goes. It seems to take forever for anything to happen.

But if the sun shines and the air is warm, and if you water your garden whenever the soil begins to get dry, the radishes should begin to appear in about a week from the time you planted them. The carrots may take a little longer. Neither vegetable will look like much—just a row of tiny green dots, two little leaves to each plant. But because they're in a straight line, where you planted them, you know they're your vegetables, and not weeds.

bean, coming up

The beans may pop up any time from a few days to a couple of weeks after you plant them; it depends a lot on how warm the days are, just after you plant. Each bean plant appears first as a curved green stem or neck, both ends of which are in the ground. But in half a day or a day, one end lifts out of the ground; it still has the bean on it, somewhat shrunk now, and two leaves opening out from inside it.

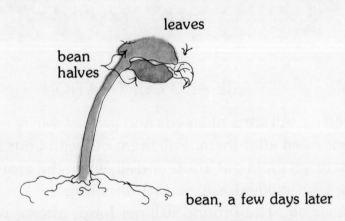

leaves

bean halves

bean, a few days later

How much should you water now? Once the seedlings are well up out of the ground, water only as often as you must to keep the soil dark and moist-looking. Don't let the soil get hard and baked out by the sun; that could kill the seedlings. But don't keep them soaking. Every second or third day is about right, if you water the garden well each time. And, of course, in cloudy weather you won't need to water that often, and in rainy weather not at all.

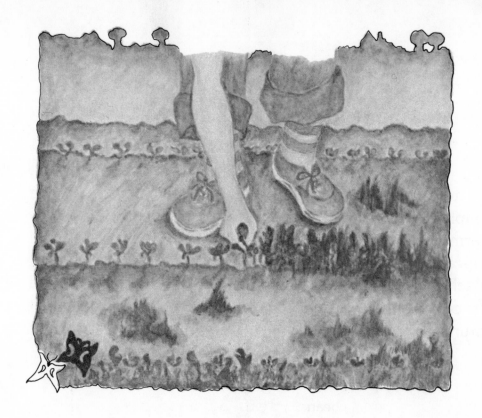

CARE AND CULTIVATION

Weeding. All sorts of weeds and grasses will sprout in your garden. Keep after them. Pull them out with your fingers (it's easiest to get them out, roots and all, when the ground is wet), or use your cultivator to scratch them up.

Cultivating. The ground will get hard, after a while, from being wet and drying out. So about once every couple of weeks, use your cultivator to loosen the soil on both sides of the rows of radishes and carrots, and around each circle of beans. This will help water and air to reach the roots. But don't dig deep or get close to your plants, because you'll damage their roots with the cultivator if you do. Stay a hand's width away from them, and cultivate only the top inch or so of the soil.

Thinning. Every gardener puts in too many seeds, because they don't all sprout. But once they've started coming up, they will probably be crowded and too close together. Yet every plant needs room or it won't grow properly, so as soon as the radishes and carrots are about an inch high, pull out some of them until there is only one plant every two inches. Like this:

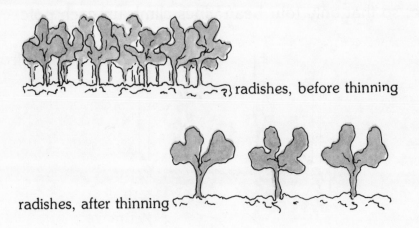

radishes, before thinning

radishes, after thinning

As for the beans, when they begin to grow you'll see that they reach out with long, thin feelers or *tendrils*, trying to find something to climb on. They'll get hold of the poles by themselves and start to wind around and up them, but if they don't, you can help them by gently guiding each tendril

around the pole. Be sure to go counterclockwise, or backward from the way a clock's hands move, because that's how they want to go. About the time the beans are beginning to reach for the pole, pull out the two weakest or smallest ones in each circle, so that only four bean vines climb up each pole.

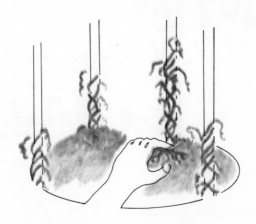

Side dressing. When your beans are higher than your knees but not quite up to your hip, it's time to give them some more plant food. Use less than you did the first time, and scatter it on the ground all around each circle, a little way outside it. At the same time, sprinkle a little on each side of your row of carrots. As for the radishes, by this time you're probably pulling them up and eating them, so wait until you replant the row with new seeds, and at that time add a little fresh fertilizer on each side of the row.

Insecticides. No poison sprays in your garden, please! One of the best things about growing your own vegetables is that you know they're safe. Insects probably won't bother you, anyhow, since all three of your crops are resistant to them. But if you do get tiny white flies in your bean vines or you see holes appearing in the leaves or bean pods, mix up some soapy water and sprinkle it over them. Or buy a spray containing *pyrethrum* —a natural plant substance that is not poisonous to human beings or animals, but only to insects.

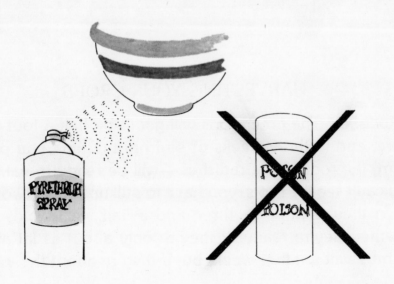

HARVESTING YOUR CROPS

Radishes. The green tops will get to be half a foot tall, or more, and in three weeks or so from the time you planted them, the roots—the radishes—will be ready to eat. Since you can't see the roots, you have to pull up one or two plants when they're three or three and a half weeks old, to see whether they're ready. If they're only about as fat as your thumb, wait another week, but if they're about the size of a

Ping-Pong ball, they're ready. Don't leave them in the ground too long; they become very hot in flavor. You can pull them all up when they're ready, and cut off the leafy tops and wash and store the radishes in the refrigerator. They'll keep for a week or two if you put them in a plastic bag. Sow a fresh crop as soon as the first one is gone.

Carrots. The tops grow a fine feathery bunch of green leaves. When they're about half a foot tall or a little taller, the roots will be starting to develop into carrots. At this point, you must thin them out a second time, so that they're about four inches apart. Four inches is the distance from

here   to   here.

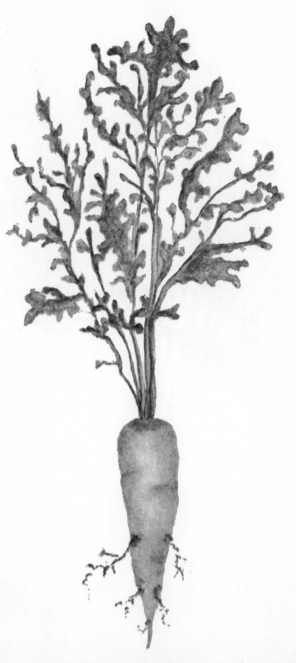

As you pull up some plants to leave room for the others, those you pull up will be baby, tender carrots; they're delicious, so wash them and eat them. But let the others stay in the ground until the tops are a foot or more tall and two months have passed since you planted them. Then pull up one or two to see

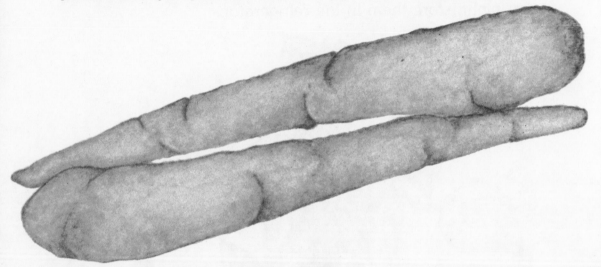

if they're fully grown; they should be almost as long as this page is wide. If they're ready, you can pull up enough for a meal, each time, or you can pull them all up, cut off the leafy tops, and wash and store them in the refrigerator as you did the radishes.

Beans. Your beans will grow so fast it almost seems you can see them growing. Round and round the poles they wind, and among the leaves you'll see many tiny flowers appearing. Where each flower is, a bean will grow. At first, they're skinny little green threads, but in a few days each bean grows longer and fatter. They hang straight down together in clumps. When they're about ¾ as long as this page is wide, pull them off gently, one at a time. You can pick enough for a meal for a family of four in a few minutes. Don't let them stay on the vines after they've reached eating size, because they get too big and tough. Also, if the beans stay on the vine, the plant stops making more—but if you keep picking, it will keep turning out new beans for you for many weeks. So pick beans as soon as they're ready, and if you don't need them that night, store them in the refrigerator.

THE END — AND THE BEGINNING

Now you've come to the end of this story of what your first season as a vegetable gardener will be like. But the end of the first season won't really be an end — it will be a beginning of a lifetime of pleasure from gardening and growing your own food. And in following years you'll be able to grow many other vegetables, some as easy as these, others more complicated. Usually, the seed packages tell you most of what you need to know about how to take care of the plants.

And although you've come to the end of this book, it's time to turn back to page one and begin.

Let's go!